21.99

in
the
news™

MODERN-DAY SLAVERY

Linda Bickerstaff

ROSEN
PUBLISHING®

New York

Published in 2010 by The Rosen Publishing Group, Inc.
29 East 21st Street, New York, NY 10010

Copyright © 2010 by The Rosen Publishing Group, Inc.

First Edition

Library of Congress Cataloging-in-Publication Data

Bickerstaff, Linda.
Modern-day slavery / Linda Bickerstaff. — 1st ed.
     p. cm. — (In the news)
Includes bibliographical references and index.
ISBN-13: 978-1-4358-5274-7 (library binding)
ISBN-13: 978-1-4358-5554-0 (pbk)
ISBN-13: 978-1-4358-5555-7 (6 pack)
1. Slavery. 2. Human trafficking. 3. Forced labor. I. Title.
HT857.B43 2010
306.3'62 — dc22

                                                                    2008055477

Manufactured in the United States of America

On the cover: Top left: Ghanian slave girls labor in the marketplace of Ghana's capital city, Accra. Rape and other forms of abuse are a part of their everyday lives. Top right: Recently freed from slavery herself, this young girl participates in a freedom march meant to highlight the plight of child slaves throughout the world. Bottom: This slave girl was sold to the owner of a brick-making factory in India.

contents

The Basics of Slavery

Speak the word "slave" and some people see African men loading bales of cotton onto paddleboats on the Mississippi River. Maybe the word calls to mind a terrified young black woman named Eliza, escaping with her son across the ice-blocked Ohio River in Harriet Beecher Stowe's antislavery novel, *Uncle Tom's Cabin*. What most people don't picture when they think of slavery are hundreds of child slaves making carpets in India or young girls and women chained to sewing machines in sweatshops in California. These children and women—and millions of others—are modern-day slaves.

Who Are Slaves?

Anti-Slavery International, a human rights organization, defines a slave as:

- A person who is forced to work by threat of mental or physical abuse

The South Asian Coalition on Child Servitude estimates that between two hundred thousand and three hundred thousand children are enslaved in the woolen carpet industry in central India alone.

- A person who is owned or controlled by another person
- A person who is dehumanized and treated like a commodity (an item that is bought or sold) or as property
- A person who is physically constrained and has no freedom of movement

Stated another way, slaves are people who are bought, kidnapped, or victimized by others and forced to work whether they want to or not. Slaves are not paid, or they are paid very little. They are given just enough food to stay alive. If they don't work, they are threatened with punishment, beaten, or abused. They are prevented from going where they want to go. Some are even locked up or chained.

The word "slavery" is often interchanged with the words "human trafficking." Many authors use them to mean the same thing. In this book, human trafficking means slave trading, not slavery itself. People who are trafficked are bought, kidnapped, or taken by a person called a trafficker or slave trader. The trafficker then sells them to another person who enslaves them.

Would You Want This Job?

When a person applies for a job, he or she is usually given a job description. It tells what the employer is looking for in an employee, what the qualifications for the job are, and what the salary and other benefits of the job will be. This helps applicants know whether they are qualified for the job and also gives them an idea of whether or not the job is one they would enjoy.

In an article on modern-day slavery, the *New Internationalist* posted the following job description for slavery:

Job Description

- Sex: male or female; any age from four until death
- Characteristics: poor and vulnerable; minorities where applicable
- Hours: up to 20 a day, sometimes more
- Days per week: up to 7; 365 days a year
- Holidays: none
- Sick leave: none
- Health and safety provision: none
- Pay: below the minimum wage, often nothing
- Accommodation: basic, often provided in lieu of pay or deducted from it.

Even in today's economy, with unemployment reaching record highs, no one would apply for the job described here. Unfortunately, modern-day slaves get their jobs without even applying.

What Types of Slavery Are There?

Kevin Bales is a professor of sociology at the University of Surrey, Roehampton in London, England, and is an expert on slavery and slave trading. In his book *Disposable People: New Slavery in the Global Economy*, Bales says that there are three main categories of slavery based on the ways in which people become slaves.

These Guarani people are held in debt bondage in Bolivia. They are forced to spend more money for their lodging and food than they are paid for their back-breaking work. They are never able to pay off their debts.

The first category is chattel slavery. The word "chattel" means any item of movable or immovable property. Chattel slaves are people who are bought or kidnapped by slave traders and then sold to slave owners. They become the property—or chattel—of their masters. Slaves in the United States prior to the Civil War were chattel slaves. They were bought from slave traders and became the property of slave owners.

The second category of slavery includes people held in debt bondage. People who are enslaved through debt bondage borrow money or incur a debt in some other way. They work for the people from whom they borrowed, but they are never able to pay off their debts because of the dishonesty of their employers. A person who controls people in debt bondage is known as a slave-holder, rather than a slave owner.

Dr. Bales's third category is contract slavery. An ABC News report tells the story of José Martinez, a Mexican man who made an agreement with someone known as a coyote. He paid the coyote to smuggle him into the United States. Martinez wanted to work and send money home to his impoverished family. However, when the coyote got him across the border, he sold Martinez to a slaveholder for $350. José Martinez is an example of a contract slave. He was forced to work in a slave camp in Florida picking tomatoes. At night he was locked in a trailer with twenty-eight other workers. He was watched by armed guards and was frequently threatened with violence. Martinez received no pay. After four months of captivity, he was able to escape.

Other classifications of slavery include forced prostitution (sex slavery), forced labor, and the worst forms of child labor. Sex slaves are usually young girls who are kidnapped or are sold by their parents to the owners of brothels (houses of prostitution). Once enslaved, the girls are forced to have sexual intercourse with many men. If they refuse or try to leave the brothel, they are punished. Boys and adult women may also be forced into prostitution.

Forced labor is the type of slavery in which political authorities or government officials force people to work without payment. The people are usually forced to work in harsh and hazardous conditions.

In child labor, children who have been kidnapped, given away, or sold by their parents are forced to work very long hours for no pay. They are poorly fed, they may be locked up or chained, and they may be beaten. The International Labor Organization (ILO), a United Nations group, defines "worst forms of child labor" as the forced recruitment of children for:

- Use in armed conflicts (child soldiers)
- Use as prostitutes (sex slaves)
- Use in the performance and production of pornography
- Use in the manufacture and/or trafficking of drugs
- Use in other work that puts a child's health, safety, or morals at risk

The ILO estimates that in 2000, 352 million children between the ages of five and seventeen worked worldwide. Not all of them were slaves, but many were. An ILO conference held in 1999 adopted a set of measures to prohibit and eliminate the worst forms of child labor.

When Did Slavery Start?

Slavery probably began when agricultural practices started about twelve thousand years ago. Slavery was present in all ancient cultures. For example, slaves were critical to the economic well-being of ancient Greece and the Roman Empire. Evidence of slavery has also been found in Mayan and Aztec ruins. Slavery was not uncommon among Native American tribes.

Slavery in Africa existed for centuries before the Atlantic slave trade began in 1510. Over the four centuries of the Atlantic slave trade, eleven million African slaves were transported to the Americas or the Caribbean Islands. Of the eleven million, 5 percent (about 550,000) were brought to North America.

Although most of the slaves brought to the American colonies worked in the South, slavery was legal in all thirteen colonies before the Revolutionary War (1775–1783). After the war, most of the newly independent states banned the slave trade and the northern states made slavery illegal. The Constitutional Convention of 1787 would have been the perfect opportunity to eliminate slavery in the United States. Unfortunately, that didn't happen. Twelve of the thirteen states voted to do so, but South Carolina refused to give up legal slavery and eventually swayed the convention. Slavery was a major issue of dispute between the

This sketch, drawn by a British visitor to the United States in 1833, shows a slave trader auctioning off chattel slaves at a market in Charleston, South Carolina.

northern and southern states over the next forty-five years. It was also one of the major issues that led to the American Civil War (1861–1865).

Legal slavery in the United States was abolished at the end of the Civil War by the passage of the Thirteenth Amendment to the U.S. Constitution in 1865. It took 115 more years for legal slavery to be abolished in the rest of the world. Mauritania was the last country to declare slavery illegal, which it did in 1980. Unfortunately, despite the law, slavery still flourishes there and throughout the world.

Why Does Modern-Day Slavery Exist?

In his book *Disposable People*, Kevin Bales says that modern slavery exists because of three factors. The first factor is the worldwide population explosion. Since the end of World War II, the world's population has increased from 2 billion to 5.7 billion people.

Rapid social and economic change is the second factor contributing to the development of modern-day slavery. As developing countries modernized, many people lost the small farms and businesses that sustained them. They became desperately poor while the elite became richer.

Corrupt governments, organized crime, and dishonest individuals combine to form the third factor leading to the new slavery. These groups and individuals prey upon poor and vulnerable people and enslave them.

Slavery in the United States

Many Americans are unaware of the existence of modern-day slavery in the United States. To some extent, this is a result of the country's memory of "historical" slavery. The slavery most Americans know was brought to North America by European colonists. It ended after the Civil War with the passage of the Thirteenth Amendment to the U.S. Constitution. Americans can't see "new" slavery because it is so different from "old" slavery. In spite of the ignorance of most Americans about it—or an unwillingness to recognize that it is taking place— modern-day slavery does exist in the United States.

The Modern Slave Trade Is Flourishing

Slave trading—or human trafficking, as it is now called— flourishes worldwide, including in the United States. The U.S. State Department estimates that between six hundred thousand and eight hundred thousand slaves

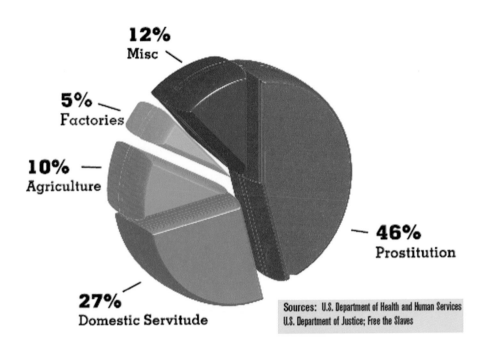

12%
Misc

5%
Factories

10%
Agriculture

46%
Prostitution

27%
Domestic Servitude

Sources: U.S. Department of Health and Human Services
U.S. Department of Justice; Free the Slaves

Although the actual number is not known, the U.S. Central Intelligence Agency estimates that between 14,500 and 17,500 slaves are trafficked into the United States each year. Almost half of these people are girls and women trafficked as sex slaves.

are trafficked worldwide each year. The United Nations estimates this number to be about seven hundred thousand. Eighty percent of these slaves are women and children. It is unclear how many of these people are brought into the United States and then enslaved.

In a *New York Times* article in 2000, reporter Joel Brinkley discussed a Central Intelligence Agency (CIA) report, "International Trafficking in Women to the United States: A Contemporary Manifestation of Slavery," that was never released to the public. In the report, the CIA estimated that about 50,000 people are brought into the United States each year and enslaved. Jerry Markon, a *Washington Post* staff writer, questioned the accuracy of this report. He wrote that the CIA estimate was "an unscientific estimate by a CIA analyst who relied mainly on clippings from foreign newspapers." In 2004, the CIA reduced its estimate to a number between 14,500 and 17,500.

The actual number of modern-day slaves in the United States will probably never be known. As Tony Fratto, deputy press secretary under President George W. Bush said, the issue is "not about the numbers. It's really about the crime and how horrific it is."

The modern slave trade is a very lucrative, or profitable, business. It is the third most profitable criminal enterprise in the world following drug trafficking and the illegal sale of arms and munitions. The United Nations Office on Drugs and Crime estimates that the total market value of human trafficking worldwide is $32 billion yearly. Ten billion dollars is made from the initial sale of slaves. The remaining value comes from the services performed and the goods made by slaves. The American Anti-Slavery Group, in its article "Modern Slavery 101" states, "Experts estimate trafficking in the U.S. yields $9 billion every year."

The United States is a popular destination country for slave trading. The CIA, in its 2000 report, listed several reasons for its popularity:

- Slave traders are at low risk for prosecution (legal action) in the United States.
- Slaves can be bought cheaply abroad and sold for large amounts in America.
- The United States has a good infrastructure for international transportation.
- Organized crime has a strong foothold in America.

Except for the first reason, all of these points hold true today. In 2000, Congress passed the Trafficking Victims Protection Act. Traffickers are now prosecuted for their crimes more frequently, and they are getting stiffer sentences than they did before 2000.

Slave trading and slavery in the United States may be lucrative for traffickers and slaveholders, but they are expensive for U.S. taxpayers. Jerry Markon reports that the government spent $28.5 million in 2006 to fight human trafficking within the United States.

Evidence of Slavery in the United States

There is ample evidence in the news that slavery exists in the United States. Long before the Trafficking Victims Protection Act existed, human rights abuses related to slavery were discovered in the United States.

Jesse Sage, associate director of the American Anti-Slavery Group, reports that in 1978, the Federal

Bureau of Investigation (FBI) encountered what it called "the first classic case of slavery in the United States this century." The victim was Rose Iftony, a young girl from Sierra Leone. She was a domestic slave in the home of a Pakistani couple in Miami, Florida. As with many modern-day slaves, Rose came to the United States with the understanding that she would have a paying job. The couple who enslaved Rose did not pay her, kept her confined in the house, and forced her to work long hours. They controlled her by threatening to contact authorities, who would send her back to Sierra Leone because she did not have a passport or a work permit.

Another report of slavery was in the news in 1995. In August of that year, immigration officials raided a clothing manufacturing workshop in El Monte, California. Seventy-two Thai women were trapped inside, working sixteen-hour days sewing clothes to be sold in stores such as Macy's, Filene's, and Hecht's. These women were held in debt bondage because they could not repay the factory owners for the cost of their transportation to America. Their children were held as hostages. Two workers who tried to escape were beaten and sent back to Thailand.

WCBS-TV in New York aired a story on December 17, 2007, about another case of modern-day slavery. Mahender Murlidhar Sabhnani and his wife, Varsha, had just been found guilty of forced labor, conspiracy, involuntary

August 2005 marked the tenth anniversary of the freeing of seventy-two Thai slaves from a sweatshop in California. The women pictured here were four of those slaves.

servitude, and harboring aliens. The millionaire couple hired two Indonesian women as housekeepers in 2002 and proceeded to enslave them. One of the women said that Mrs. Sabhnani scalded, sliced, clubbed, cut, and pinched her. The couple also starved her at times and on one occasion, forced her to eat one hundred chili peppers. A follow-up story on WNBC News on June 26, 2008, reported that Mrs. Sabhnani received an eleven-year jail sentence to be followed by three years of probation and the payment of $25,000 in fines. Mr. Sabhnani received a three-and-a-half-year jail sentence and a $12,500 fine.

Enung, an Indonesian woman, was held as a domestic slave by a wealthy New York couple. The mat on which she is seen here was allegedly the only sleeping accommodation she was given.

Another case of modern-day slavery was reported by Russell Goldman on ABC News on June 19, 2008. A federal grand jury indicted a former judge, William Garrett; his deputy sheriff son, Russell; and the son's wife, Malika, for human trafficking, alien harboring, witness tampering, and making false statements. In January 2003, Malika Garrett returned to her native India for a visit. When she came back to the United States, she brought a young Indian woman with her to work as a nanny. The nanny was never paid. She lived in an unfinished and unheated basement room. She was forced to work sixteen hours a day and was threatened with physical violence. She was told that if she tried to alert authorities to her plight, she would be accused of being a terrorist. As of this writing, no court dates have been set for this trial.

Not all slaves in the United States are trafficked from abroad. The *Arizona Republic* ran a story about a fifteen-year-old American girl who was enslaved. The girl ran away from home and had the great misfortune of running into eighteen-year-old Matthew Gray and nineteen-year-old Jannelle Butler. The couple bound the girl and took her to a nearby apartment where she was sexually abused. Over the following month, the girl was psycho-logically abused, kept in a cramped dog kennel, and sold into prostitution on an Internet site. She was eventually rescued by police, who had been contacted by the girl's mother at the time of her disappearance. Gray and Butler were charged with sexual assault, kidnapping, receiving earnings from a prostitute, and other charges.

All of these cases show that modern-day slavery is indeed active in the United States. New cases are mentioned almost daily in newspapers across the country. Fortunately, the American public is becoming more aware of this ongoing problem and is starting to take the steps necessary to stop it.

Slavery is universal. It is practiced in every country in the world. There are, however, countries, or areas within countries, that appear to be hot spots for the practice of specific types of slavery.

Chattel Slavery in Mauritania

Long before slaves were brought to America, chattel slavery was practiced in Mauritania. In chattel slavery, slaves become the property of their masters. This kind of slavery is still practiced in Mauritania today.

Mauritania is located just south of Morocco in northwest Africa and has a population of 3.3 million people. Thirty to forty percent of Mauritanians are Caucasian Muslims (followers of Islam). The remaining two million people are black Africans, and almost all of them are also Muslims. Of the black Mauritanians, nearly five hundred thousand are slaves or former slaves.

Slavery was declared illegal in Mauritania in 1980 and was criminalized in 2007. Despite this, it still occurs.

Most slave owners in Mauritania are members of large extended families and are descendents of white Muslim people. The ancestors of many of the black African slaves in Mauritania, who were also slaves, converted to Islam centuries ago. This creates one of the bizarre aspects of slavery in Mauritania. The Qur'an—the Islamic holy book—forbids Muslims to enslave other Muslims, and yet in Mauritania they do. Because they are Muslims, many slaves believe that they were placed in the service of their masters by the will of God. These slaves believe that leaving their masters would be a grave sin. This religious belief has enabled slave owners to hold their slaves with little need for violent coercion.

An article in the *Washington Post* tells the story of Boubacar Messaoud, a former slave who is the founder of the antislavery group SOS Slaves. According to local practice, because he was a slave, he was not permitted to go to school. This condition persists for slaves today. Of the five hundred thousand slaves in

This Mauritanian child, photographed in 2007, is probably the descendant of chattel slaves.

Mauritania, 80 percent do not have access to formal education. Messaoud was fortunate that a sympathetic school principal shamed his master into allowing him to go to school. He was the first in his family to do so. He managed to make his way through college and become an architect. Now he fights for the freedom of all slaves through his organization, SOS Slaves.

Debt Bondage in India and Pakistan

Debt bondage is the least known and the most widely used method of enslaving people worldwide. Between fifteen million and twenty million people are held in debt bondage around the world. In this form of slavery, a person (the debtor) pledges himself to someone else against a loan of money. The length and nature of the service required of the debtor are never clearly defined. The debtor's labor does not reduce the original debt because the slaveholder is dishonest in his bookkeeping. In addition, the debtor must buy food, lodging, and other necessities of life from the slaveholder. These costs often exceed what the person earns, so he becomes more deeply indebted. This debt is passed on to future generations.

Debt bondage in Pakistan's brick industry is one example of this type of slavery. There are about seven thousand functioning brick kilns in Pakistan with an annual production of as many as sixty-five billion bricks. To do the work, 150,000 to 200,000 families, or about 700,000 people, are held in debt bondage in almost intolerable conditions. Many of the brickworkers were displaced from their farms when the government and large businesses took their land. They borrowed money, sometimes as little as fifteen or twenty dollars, and agreed to pay it back by working in the kilns. Families of brickworkers make as many as 8,500 bricks a week for which they are paid seven hundred to eight hundred rupees (about fourteen to sixteen dollars). That is almost exactly what kiln owners charge for food and housing per family. Therefore, the debt is never paid off. The owners of the kilns (the slaveholders) have various ways to intimidate workers who they believe are slacking off. Kiln owners may break all of the bricks a family makes in a day or punish a worker by putting his legs into the kiln. Some owners sexually abuse female brickworkers.

Debt bondage is also common among agricultural workers in India. In his book *Disposable People*, Kevin Bales tells of Shivraj, a man held in debt bondage. Shivraj's grandfather and father both incurred debts by borrowing money to buy grain to plant. Shivraj says, "I've always been here, so were my father and grandfather. We've always been here and we've always worked for the same master. When my father died, I had to take over his debt. That was almost thirty years ago. When he

This man and his children are among the thousands of slaves held in debt bondage in Pakistan. The family works making bricks to try to pay off their debts. They will probably remain in debt bondage for generations to come.

died he owed the master 1,200 rupees ($33), a lot of money!" Shivraj managed to pay off all but 200 rupees (about $6) of the debt before a drought led to a crop failure. He had to borrow money for more seed and is still in debt bondage.

Forced Prostitution in Thailand

Charles Jacobs, president of the American Anti-Slavery Group, reports on the group's Web site, iAbolish.org, that hundreds of thousands of children, both girls and boys, have been kidnapped, tricked, or sold and delivered to brothels. This is especially true in Thailand, where more than thirty-five thousand individuals live as sex slaves. Local men and men from abroad visit the brothels and pay for the child prostitutes. An entire industry of sex tourism has developed in Thailand, in which Western and Japanese men travel to the country for the prostitution. It is important to the economy of the country, so little has been done to eradicate it.

Sex slavery is now so ingrained in Thai culture that many sex slaves accept their fate as just another way of life. Sex slaves are forced to have sexual relations with many men each night, receive little if any money, and are frequently kept in locked compounds. If they try to escape, they are hunted down and returned by corrupt policemen who are paid by the brothel owners. If sex slaves develop AIDS, which most of them eventually do, they are thrown out to fend for themselves.

Sex slavery occurs in the United States as well. A *New York Times* article tells the story of Na, a twenty-three-year-old Thai woman who was tricked into coming to the United States, at no cost to her, by a man who offered her a job as a bar hostess. When she arrived in New York, she found out the truth. Her employers required her to pay back the cost of her ticket and other expenses by having sexual relations with hundreds of men. She was held captive in a Chinatown brothel with barred windows. She was not allowed to leave the building until she had worked off her debt. Na was rescued from forced prostitution when police raided the brothel.

Forced Labor in Myanmar and the Dominican Republic

Forced labor is used by some as an umbrella term for all forms of slavery. It also has a specific meaning. It is labor required by a government or by agencies of a government. The workers are paid nothing. They are forced to work in very harsh conditions and are punished if they do not work. People who have been convicted of crimes and forced to work as part of their punishment are not included in this classification.

Forced labor, like all forms of slavery, has been declared illegal in numerous international agreements and by orders of the United Nations. However, it is still used by corrupt governments in Myanmar (Burma), the Dominican Republic, and other countries. According to an article in the *New Statesman*, the military in Myanmar routinely forces civilians to work for no pay on projects like building roads, bridges, military bases, and even towns. If individuals refuse to work, they are threatened, harassed, beaten, and occasionally, killed. In describing one particularly brutal example of forced labor, the author reports, "villagers are used as human minesweepers to clear the way for the safe passage of soldiers."

The Dominican Republic uses forced labor to harvest its sugarcane crop. The slaves who do this work come from neighboring Haiti, one of the poorest countries in the world. According to Charles Jacobs, many Haitians willingly work on Dominican sugar plantations. During harvest time, however, there are not enough workers so Dominican soldiers fan out across the country and arrest any Haitians they can find to help with the harvest.

Slaves forced into labor by the government in Myanmar do heavy and dangerous work, such as carrying baskets of stone for road construction.

Marc Pierre, a twenty-four-year-old Haitian man, tells of his experience on the Web site iAbolish.org. After Pierre crossed the border on a shopping trip to the Dominican Republic, a soldier arrested and jailed him. Pierre says, "When I told him I didn't want to cut cane, he hit me with his rifle." Pierre, along with other detainees, was held in filthy barracks at a military post. When enough Haitians had been rounded up, they were driven to a shantytown at the edge of a sugar plantation. All of Pierre's belongings were confiscated. He was handed a machete and told to get to work. He was told that if he wanted to eat he had to work, and he was threatened with a beating if he tried to escape. Marc Pierre was not paid for his work.

Worst Forms of Child Labor in India and Other Countries

India's carpet slaves fall into the category of the worst forms of child labor. An article on iAbolish.org tells the story of five-year-old Santosh, an East Indian boy. One day, while he was playing with friends, a group of men offered to take the children to a movie. The children got into the jeep and away they went—400 miles (643.7 kilometers) away and into slavery. Santosh made carpets for nine years, working from four in the morning until eleven at night, seven days a week, without breaks. When he cut his finger, the loom master shaved sulfur from match heads and set it on fire to stop the bleeding. He didn't want his carpets soiled with blood. When Santosh was finally rescued, he was underweight and underdeveloped. He was very withdrawn and would not communicate with anyone.

As many as three hundred thousand children work in the carpet industry in India alone. There are five hundred thousand children working in Pakistan and probably as many as two hundred thousand in Nepal.

Child slaves work at other jobs as well. In an article for the Anti-Slavery Society (Australia), Melanie Gow reported that in 2002, more than three hundred thousand children were taking part in approximately thirty-six armed conflicts (wars) around the world. Child soldiers are people under the age of eighteen who are members of any armed group. They may be cooks, porters, messengers, or fighters. Girls are often recruited as sex slaves, but they may also work in other capacities—even as fighters.

It is estimated that as many as one million children work as slaves in the carpet industry. Their nimble fingers and good eyesight make them valuable to slaveholders.

Myanmar is one of the worst offenders. Human rights groups estimate that there are more than seventy thousand child soldiers in the Myanmar army. Carole Reckinger reports in the *New Statesman* that children in Myanmar are often kidnapped on their way home from school. They are brutalized and physically abused during induction into the army and, after basic training, they are shipped off to fight in the country's ethnic wars. They are forced to participate in killing, burning villages, and other atrocities. Many child soldiers try to desert the army, but if caught, they are beaten and forced to return to the army or they are imprisoned.

Combating Modern-Day Slavery

There are no quick "fixes" for modern-day slavery. Slavery will not be eliminated until overpopulation and poverty are controlled and until slavery is no longer profitable for slaveholders and slave traffickers. Meanwhile, slavery is being fought internationally, nationally, by state and local governments, by many nongovernmental organizations (NGOs), and by concerned individuals. This fight takes many forms in the United States.

Fighting Slavery with Legislation

The federal government has enacted numerous laws making slavery illegal in the United States. During the Civil War, President Abraham Lincoln issued the Emancipation Proclamation, which freed the slaves in states that had seceded from, or left, the Union and joined the Confederacy. It did not free slaves owned by people in states that remained in the Union. At the end of the war, members of Congress wanted to make sure that all slaves were free, so they drafted the Thirteenth Amendment to the Constitution. It was ratified (approved) in 1865.

The Thirteenth Amendment was the first legislation that specifically prohibited all slavery. The amendment states, "Neither slavery or involuntary servitude, except as punishment for crime, whereof the party shall have been duly convicted, shall exist within the United States or any place subject to their jurisdiction." In other words, no person's freedom can be taken away from him or her by another person. It also means that a person cannot be forced to work if he or she chooses not to. The exception is a person who is convicted of a crime. That person may be required to work as part of the punishment for committing the crime. The amendment prohibits slavery throughout the United States and in countries or territories controlled by the United States, such as Puerto Rico and Guam.

Today, all laws that are passed by the United States Congress are recorded in what is called the U.S. Code. Title 18 of the U.S. Code deals with crime and criminal procedures. Section 1581 of Title 18 makes it illegal to force a person to work through debt servitude. Section 1584 makes it a crime to force a person to work against his or her will. This applies to any situation where the force is violence, the threat of violence, the threat of legal

Condoleezza Rice, as U.S. secretary of state, was a spokesperson for the fight against modern-day slavery throughout the world.

action, or "a climate of fear" (any situation that makes a person very afraid). New laws against slavery will be added to the next revision of the code.

In 2000, Congress passed the Trafficking Victims Protection Act. This law established the Office to Monitor and Combat Trafficking in Persons in the U.S. State Department. It also instructed the Department of Health and Human Services to develop resources to protect and assist rescued slaves. In addition, it provided for the development of T-visas to help rescued slaves stay in the United States. T-visas treat slaves as victims of a crime rather than as illegal aliens to be deported (legally sent) back to their countries. Those who receive T-visas may stay in the United States for three years and may qualify for permanent residency.

A *Los Angeles Times* article reported the story of Thonglim Khamphiranon to illustrate how T-visas work. Khamphiranon, a single mother trying to support two children in Thailand, accepted a job cooking in a Thai restaurant in Los Angeles. When she arrived in the United States, her employer enslaved her. She eventually escaped. In order to qualify for a T-visa, Khamphiranon had to 1) prove that she was the victim of a "severe form" of trafficking; 2) prove that she would face "extreme hardship" if deported; and 3) cooperate with requests from law enforcement agencies who investigated and brought legal action against her employer. She complied with all of these requirements and received a T-visa. Her employer was convicted and sentenced to eight years in a federal prison.

Victim advocates—those who work to help crime victims—believe the requirements for a T-visa are too demanding. They say that victims may not want to work with law enforcement because they are too traumatized (mentally or emotionally injured), distrust the police, or fear deportation. Government officials, on the other hand, say a victim's willingness to work with law enforcement is essential. Wade Horn, an assistant secretary with the Department of Health and Human Services, stated in the *New York Times*, "If we are going to abolish modern-day slavery, then we have to put the traffickers out of business. That's going to demand, unfortunately, the cooperation of the victims."

Mark P. Lagon, director of the Office to Monitor and Combat Trafficking in Persons, gave an address to a

United Nations forum in February 2008. He gave an excellent summary of what the United States is doing to fight trafficking at home. He reported that since 2000, there have been many revisions to the Trafficking Victims Protection Act and that the changes have taken the victims' needs into account. As a result, far fewer victims are being deported. According to Lagon, victims are being treated with care, "allowing them to become survivors of this traumatic crime." The United States issued more than two thousand T-visas between January 2001 and January 2008.

Another program at the federal level is the Rescue and Restore campaign begun by the Department of Health and Human Services in 2004. This campaign established the National Human Trafficking Resource Center, whose primary job is to educate the public about slavery and to aid its victims. The center developed a hotline for both reporting slavery and seeking help. Over an eighteen-month period, the hotline received four thousand calls, leading to 120 cases for investigation.

Direct Action Programs Fight Slavery

In spite of federal and state laws against human trafficking, prosecution of traffickers—or putting traffickers on trial—has been difficult and questionably effective in fighting slavery. Proving that a person has been trafficked,

Teens are warned of the dangers of modern-day slavery through MTV EXIT. The program supports a Web site (http://www.mtvexit.org/eng/index_flash.html) that provides facts about modern-day slavery for young people worldwide. Pictured above is the English language page of the site.

as opposed to smuggled, into the United States is the main stumbling block to convicting traffickers, or proving them guilty in a court of law. According to an article in the *Seattle Post-Intelligencer*, between 2001 and 2005, the U.S. Justice Department investigated 555 people suspected of slave trading. Only 75 criminals were convicted. There is obviously a need to approach the fight against slavery from other angles and not to rely only on law enforcement efforts. The following two direct action programs are examples of other ways to fight slavery.

MTV Fights Slavery

The U.S. Agency for International Development (USAID) and the MTV Europe Foundation is partnering with MTV on a campaign to educate young people about the dangers of human trafficking. The program, called MTV EXIT (End Exploitation and Trafficking), focuses especially on South Asia and the Asia Pacific region, where slave trading is most prevalent. Internet users can log on to an engrossing, informative Web site available in twenty-seven languages. The purpose is to reach young people around the world—many of whom watch MTV—to warn them that they are at risk of enslavement. This program is expected to reach three hundred million households in South Asia and the Asia Pacific regions.

MTV EXIT has produced two documentaries to raise awareness of slavery and slave trafficking: *Sold* and *Traffic*. Both films contain cold, hard facts about slavery and slave trading. The documentaries tell the stories of real people who were sold and trafficked. The documentaries also look at people who are trying to help victims and explore the challenges they face. Radiohead, a popular music group, joined the campaign in April 2008, making a music video for a song called "All I Need." The group's video looks at child labor, another form of slavery.

Texas Hold 'Em Fights Slavery

In the *Austin American-Statesman*, Bob Keefe reports on a program that was announced by Rick Perry, the governor of Texas. The program, dubbed Texas Hold 'Em, is an effort by the U.S. Border Patrol and the Mexican government to cut down on the smuggling of Mexicans into the United States. Too often, people trying to cross the U.S.–Mexico border become the victims of those who smuggle them. They end up as slaves, working and living in horrible conditions for no pay. They are frequently physically and psychologically abused.

The program includes the development of a toll-free hotline for tipsters with rewards for information leading to criminal convictions. Since many potential slaves are trafficked by commercial truckers, the program makes it easier to revoke the driver's licenses of truckers who are convicted of smuggling. It is hoped that the program will result in zero commercial truck drivers participating in trafficking.

How American Youth Are Fighting Slavery

Young people have taken the problem of modern-day slavery and slave trading to heart. Some young people have made significant statements—and have taken important actions—against these evils.

Take Zack Hunter, for instance. Zack started his abolitionist (antislavery) activities at the age of twelve, when he first learned about modern-day slavery. He started a campaign called Loose Change to Loosen Chains, which raised more than $10,000 by having kids donate spare change to the cause. Zack has continued his abolitionist work by writing a book, *Be the Change: Your Guide to Freeing Slaves and Changing the World*. It tells the stories of kids his age or younger who became victims of slavery and slave trading.

According to an article in *Publishers Weekly*, Zack believes that his youth is an asset in his quest to help end slavery. He thinks that adults, who have the resources to support antislavery efforts, don't have the "passion" to do so. Young people, on the other hand, have plenty of passion but few resources. Zack believes that students and adults, working together to abolish slavery, would be "a deadly combination." In other words, as a team, they could be extremely effective.

According to an article in the *Jewish Journal*, Miri Cypers and Rena Stern founded the Teen Political Activist Coalition (T-PAC) as high school freshmen. Rena Stern said, "All the other clubs on campus were mainly concerned with improving the school or immediate community. We wanted to start a group which used political action to improve the world at large." After reading a newspaper article about a young woman enslaved as a domestic worker in Palos Verdes, California, not far from their homes, Miri and Rena took action. They organized a benefit concert in West Hollywood featuring several local bands. They gave the money earned from this Rockin' Against Slavery concert to the Coalition to Abolish Slavery and Trafficking (CAST).

End Slavery Now, a project started by teenage sisters Joan and Grace Park, held a conference for teens to educate them about slavery and a benefit concert. The money raised from the concert went to organizations that help trafficking victims in Minneapolis and St. Paul, Minnesota. According to an article in the *Daily Planet*, Minnesota is one of the thirteen states with the highest number of human trafficking incidents. Shortly before Joan and Grace Park organized End Slavery Now, police busted a forced prostitution ring that was holding one hundred Chinese and Korean women in debt bondage. The women were forced to work in brothels, which were poorly disguised as massage parlors, and they were not allowed to leave. Their visas and passports were taken away. They were physically and psychologically abused. Newspaper articles about this event and a program on slavery presented at their church prompted the Park sisters to find a way to help people in modern-day slavery. End Slavery Now was the way.

After Emancipation

5

s it possible to eradicate, or wipe out, slavery? Many experts believe that it is. Expert Kevin Bales recommends the following steps to end slavery:

- Slow population growth to decrease poverty and the supply of potential slaves.
- Continue to educate the public.
- Change laws to extend the responsibility for slavery to corporations and organized crime groups that benefit from it.

Will society's responsibility for slaves end when they are emancipated, or freed from slavery? Many people believe that emancipation alone is not enough.

Learning from the Past

After slaves were emancipated in the United States in 1865, no effort was made to help them. Bales believes that much of the racial unrest that still exists in America today is due to the lack of effort to rehabilitate freed slaves after the Civil War.

Countries in Africa were also devastated by the Atlantic slave trade. Many countries lost population, and their economies were ruined by the loss of their young, healthy men and women. Some economists and sociologists believe that the political and economic problems in African countries today are tied directly to slavery and to Europe's colonization of these weakened countries.

Almost 150 years after the end of the Atlantic slave trade, historical slavery is back in the news. Some Africans, including African Americans descended from slaves, are demanding reparations (money and other things to make up for hurt, loss, or damage) to compensate for more than four hundred years of enslavement and colonization. The African Reparation Movement (ARM), based in London, England, is asking for the following:

- Acknowledgement of wrongdoing from the countries and institutions that profited from slavery
- An apology from those countries and institutions
- The return of artifacts stolen from Africa and enslaved Africans
- Monetary compensation in the trillions of dollars

When Tamar Lewin reported on the issue for the *New York Times* in 2001, members of the U.S. House of Representatives had introduced legislation calling for a study of reparations every year since 1989. No action was ever taken. Those seeking reparations felt that they were making no progress, so they decided to take a different approach. A team of prominent African American lawyers, including Charles Ogletree, a professor at Harvard Law School, decided to file lawsuits seeking damages from the federal government and from companies that profited from slavery. Ogletree believed the suits would help to call attention to the differences in the ways blacks and whites are treated in America. The suits were filed and are still pending in courts today.

Some progress has been made in winning the first two demands of ARM—gaining acknowledgment of wrongdoing and gaining apologies. On July 29, 2008, CBS News aired the story "House Issues Formal Apology for Slavery." The statement of apology said, "The House [of Representatives] apologizes to African-Americans on behalf of the people of the United States, for the wrongs committed against them and their ancestors who suffered under slavery and Jim Crow." Representative Carolyn Cheeks Kilpatrick, the chairwoman of the Congressional Black Caucus, stated, "Today represents a milestone in our nation's efforts to remedy the ills of our past."

Borneti Phillips attended a rally of hundreds of black demonstrators who were speaking out for slave reparations in Washington, D.C. Phillips is the descendant of a slave brought to the United States from Uganda in 1786.

The topic of reparations will be present in the news for years to come as the pros and cons of reparation are debated and decisions about it are made.

Dealing with the Present

Recognizing the problems created in the United States and Africa by failing to support and rehabilitate freed slaves, governments and NGOs are incorporating rehabilitation and support programs into their plans for fighting modern-day slavery.

A *Scientific American* feature story in April 2002 gave several examples of these programs. In one example, a social worker had a profound impact on the lives of women held in debt bondage in a village in India. Generations before, villagers had borrowed money, and their descendents were still trying to pay off the debts. The social worker gathered ten women from the village and proposed a plan to free them—and the entire village—from debt. The ten women were to set aside a single rupee each week from the very small amount of money they were given to buy rice. After only three months, the group had raised enough money to buy one woman's freedom. She then became a paid employee who could contribute much more money to the group. It took only two months to free the next woman and one month to free the third. Soon the entire village was debt-free. The social worker had given the slaves hope, had shown them how to free one another, and had provided the support they needed to help themselves.

The United States government and many NGOs in America have also learned from the past. They are providing extensive rehabilitation programs for those freed from slavery in America. Jessica Donohue is the director of Trafficked Person Assistance at YMCA International

Services in Houston, Texas. This branch of the YMCA provides programs and services for immigrants, refugees, and victims of human trafficking. The programs include job training, cultural orientation, and many other offerings. In an interview featured on Web site vision.org, Donohue says it is essential to understand that victims of trafficking have not only been physically enslaved, but have also lost their self-esteem and dignity. To address victims' problems, the YMCA program provides for basic needs, such as food, clothing, and shelter, and also offers counseling and other services to help each individual cope and heal.

Looking to the Future

Ultimately, abolition and rehabilitation efforts will succeed if enough people commit to the effort. What can you do to help?

1. **Be an informed consumer.** The Office to Monitor and Combat Trafficking in Persons is helping to develop a list of goods believed to be produced by forced labor and child labor. If products on this list are not purchased, the companies producing them will lose money. It is hoped that these companies will then reevaluate their use of slave labor. Similarly, Co-op America currently

provides lists of fair trade and sweat-free products. The lists identify products you can buy that are not made in sweatshops.

The U.S. History II honors class of Immaculata High School in Somerville, N.J., shows what concerned students can do about child slave labor in today's society. The class publishes newsletters throughout the year covering many aspects of child slave labor. Such newsletters can be an excellent resource to help you educate yourself about products in the marketplace. For example, student Michael Forbes wrote an article entitled "Wal-Mart + Nike = Slavery." In the article, he cites news reports showing that child slave labor is being used all over the world to produce quality name brands. He and his classmates recommend that companies known to profit from the use of child slave labor be boycotted.

2. **Encourage your parents to use shareholder clout.** Many parents invest in companies by buying stock market shares. By reviewing their retirement funds and portfolios, they can eliminate stocks in companies that use slave labor. Co-op America reports that some mutual funds are working to get companies such as Wal-Mart to adopt policies ensuring that their products are not produced in

sweatshops. Co-op America publishes a Guide to Shareholder Action that provides information about mutual funds that work to improve labor practices.

3. **Write, e-mail, or call** state and federal officials to urge their involvement in supporting the fight against slavery. Question what they have done so far, and encourage them to increase their involvement.

4. **Volunteer** for local organizations fighting slavery, such as the Rescue and Restore programs.

5. **Contribute financially.** Start or participate in fund drives to support organizations dedicated to fighting slavery and rehabilitating victims of slavery.

6. **Be observant.** You can be the eyes and ears of law enforcement agencies working to stop slavery and slave trading.

7. **Be smart.** Anyone can become vulnerable to modern-day slave traders. Discuss ways to avoid becoming a slave with your friends. Three things you can do to protect yourself are:

- Stay away from drugs. Many teens become victims of slave traders when they are under the influence of drugs.
- Be suspicious of offers of jobs that sound too good to be true. Check with local authorities and the better business bureau before taking that great-sounding job.
- Value yourself. Those who have little self-esteem are especially vulnerable to exploitation—especially sexual exploitation.

Conclusion

Modern-day slavery has a firm foothold in the United States and throughout the rest of the world. Like "old" slavery, it violates the human rights of those held captive and shames those who condone it or ignore it. The freeing of modern-day slaves will occur only when those of us who are free speak out against slavery and work together to stop it. Be a modern-day emancipator!

Glossary

abolish To do away with or to eliminate.

advocate A person who speaks for or pleads the cause of another person.

alien harboring Hiding a foreign person.

busted A slang term meaning to break up or expose.

clout Power or influence.

comply To yield to or consent to something.

conspiracy An agreement between two or more people to commit an illegal act.

consumer A person who uses goods or services to satisfy his or her needs.

convict To prove or find guilty.

debtor One who owes something, such as money, to another person.

deport To exile or to send a person out of a country.

domestic Pertaining to the house; a housekeeper.

emancipation The act or process of setting or making free.

hotline A telephone number that can be called anytime, day or night, to report something or to seek help or advice.

kiln A furnace or oven used for drying and hardening earthenware such as bricks.

machete A large knife with a slightly curved blade that has a single cutting edge; it is used for cutting crops or other plants.

munitions Military supplies, especially weapons and ammunition for weapons.

portfolio A list of stocks and bonds owned by a bank or an investor.

prosecute To start and carry on a legal suit or action.

prostitute A person who exchanges sexual favors for money or other payment.

psychologically Mentally.

Qur'an The sacred book of Muslims; its contents are believed to be revelations given to the prophet Muhammad by Allah (God).

reparations The act of making amends; something done or given to make up for a wrong or injury.

rupee The monetary unit of India, Pakistan, and other countries.

self-esteem Belief in oneself; self-respect.

sweatshop A factory in which employees (or slaves) work for long hours and low wages under unhealthy conditions.

umbrella term A word or phrase that can have many meanings or that encompasses many other words or concepts.

witness tampering To bribe or otherwise influence a person to give false testimony in a trial.

For More Information

Anti-Slavery International
Thomas Clarkson House
The Stableyard
Broomgrove Road
London SW9 9TL
England
Web site: http://www.antislavery.org
Anti-Slavery International is the world's oldest international
human rights organization, founded in 1839. It works at
local, national, and international levels to eliminate slavery
around the world.

Canadian Council for Refugees
6839 Drolet #302
Montreal, QB H25 2TI
Canada
(514) 277-7223
Web site: http://www.ccrweb.ca
The Canadian Council for Refugees is a nonprofit organization
committed to the rights and protection of refugees in Canada
and around the world. This includes the protection of persons
trafficked into Canada.

Free the Slaves
1326 14th Street NW

Washington, DC 20005
(866) 324-FREE (3733)
(202) 588-1865
Web site: http://www.freetheslaves.net
Free the Slaves is a nonprofit organization whose goal is to liberate slaves around the world, to help them to rebuild their lives, and to research real-world solutions to the problem of slavery.

International Labor Organization
4, route des Morillons
CH-1211
Geneva 22
Switzerland
Web site: http://www.ilo.org/public/english/index.htm
The International Labor Organization is the United Nations specialized agency that seeks the promotion of social justice and internationally recognized human and labor rights.

Web Sites

Due to the changing nature of Internet links, Rosen Publishing has developed an online list of Web sites related to the subject of this book. This site is updated regularly. Please use this link to access the list:

http://www.rosenlinks.com/itn/slav

For Further Reading

Bales, Kevin. *Ending Slavery: How We Free Slaves Today*. Berkeley, CA: University of California Press, 2007.

Batstone, David. *Not for Sale: The Return of the Global Slave Trade—and How We Can Fight It*. New York, NY: Harper One, 2007.

Beah, Ishmael. *A Long Way Gone: Memoirs of a Boy Soldier*. New York, NY: Sarah Crighton Books, 2007.

Bok, Frances, and Edward Tivnan. *Escape from Slavery*. New York, NY: St. Martin's Press, 2003.

Fernando, Beatrice. *In Contempt of Fate*. Merrimac, MA: Bearo Publishing, 2004.

Flores, Theresa. *The Sacred Bath: An American Teen's Story of Modern Day Slavery*. Bloomington, IN: iUniverse, 2007.

Hunter, Zack. *Be the Change: Your Guide to Freeing Slaves and Changing the World*. Grand Rapids, MI: Zondervan/Youth Specialties, 2007.

Lewis, Barbara. *The Teen Guide to Global Action*. Minneapolis, MN: Free Spirit Publishing, 2007.

Myers, Walter. *The Glory Field*. New York, NY: Scholastic Paperbacks, 2008.

Skinner, Benjamin. *A Crime So Monstrous: Face to Face with Modern Day Slavery*. New York, NY: Free Press, 2008.

Bibliography

African Reparations Movement. "ARM FAQ's."
Retrieved August 17, 2008 (http://www.arm.
arc.co.uk/FAQs.html).

American Anti-Slavery Group. "Modern Slavery 101."
iAbolish.org, 2008. Retrieved July 29, 2008 (http://
www.iabolish.org/slavery_today/primer/index/html).

Anti-Slavery International. "What Is Modern Slavery?"
Retrieved August 28, 2008 (http://www.antislavery.
org/homepage/antislavery/modern.htm).

Bales, Kevin. *Disposable People: New Slavery in the
Global Economy*. Berkeley, CA: University of
California Press, 1999.

Bales, Kevin. "The Social Psychology of Modern Slavery."
Scientific American, April 24, 2002. Retrieved August
2008 (http://www.sciam.com/article.cfm?id=
the-social-psychology-of).

Boustany, Nora. "One Man's Personal Mission to
End Slavery in Mauritania." *Washington Post*,
March 23, 2008. Retrieved August 2008 (http://www.
washingtonpost.com/wp-dyn/content/article/2008/
03/22/AR2008032202206.html).

Brinkley, Joe. "Vast Trade in Forced Labor Portrayed in
CIA Report." *New York Times*, April 2, 2000. Retrieved
August 2008 (http://query.nytimes.com/

gst/fullpage.html?res=9E07E0DA173FF931A35757C0
A9669C8B63&sec=&spon=&pagewanted=all).

Butler, Bill. "Meeting the Challenge of Rescue and
Rehabilitation." Vision.org, February 2007. Retrieved
August 25, 2008 (http://www.vision.org/visionmedia/
article.aspx?id=2302).

CBS News. "House Issues Formal Apology for Slavery."
July 29, 2008. Retrieved August 18, 2008 (http://
www.cbsnews.com/stories/2008/07/29/national/
main4305876.shtml).

CBS News. "NY Couple Guilty In 'Modern Day Slavery'
Case." CBS5.com, December 17, 2007. Retrieved
August 23, 2008 (http://cbs5.com/national/New.York.
slavery.2.612450.html).

Co-op America. "Ending Sweat Shops: What You Can Do."
2005. Retrieved August 18, 2008 (http://www.coopamerica.
org/programs/sweatshops/whatyoucando/index/cfm).

Forbes, Michael. "Wal-Mart and Nike=Slavery."
Immaculata High School, Somerville, NJ. January
2003. Retrieved August 31, 2008 (http://ihscslnews.
org/view_article.php?id=115).

Goldberg, Carey. "Sex Slavery, Thailand to New York:
Thousands of Indentured Asian Prostitutes May Be
in U.S." *New York Times*, September 11, 1995.
Retrieved August 2008 (http://query.nytimes.com/
gst/fullpage.html?res=990CE5DD123FF932A2575AC
0A963958260&sec=&spon=&pagewanted=all).

Gorman, Anna. "Program to Fight Human Trafficking Is Underused." *Los Angeles Times*, December 19, 2005. Retrieved August 2008 (http://articles.latimes.com/2005/dec/19/local/me-trafficking19).

Gow, Melanie. "Child Soldiers." Anti-Slavery Society, 2002. Retrieved August 16, 2008 (http://www.anti-slaverysociety.addr.com/csoldiers1.htm).

Jacobs, Charles. "Slavery: Worldwide Evil." American Anti-Slavery Group, 2008. Retrieved August 12, 2008 (http://www.iabolish.org/slavery_today/in_depth/global-slavery.html).

Keefe, Bob. "Border Governors Set Joint Effort Against Human Trafficking." *Austin American-Statesman*, August 15, 2008. Retrieved August 2008 (http://www.statesman.com/news/content/news/stories/local/08/15/0815humantraffic.html?cxtype=rss&cxsvc=7&cxcat=52).

Lagon, Mark. "UN Global Initiative to Fight Human Trafficking." Office to Monitor and Combat Trafficking in Persons, February 13, 2008. Retrieved August 24, 2008 (http://www.state.gov/g/tip/rls/rm/2008/101260.htm).

Leach, Susan. "Slavery Is Not Dead, Just Less Recognizable." *Christian Science Monitor*, September 1, 2004. Retrieved August 2008 (http://www.csmonitor.com/2004/0901/p16s01-wogi.html).

Lewin, Tamar. "Calls for Slavery Restitution Getting Louder." *New York Times*, June 4, 2001. Retrieved August 2008 (http://query.nytimes.com/gst/fullpage.html?res=9C03E1DD153FF937A35755C0A9679C8B63).

Markon, Jarry. "Human Trafficking Evokes Outrage, Little Evidence." *Washington Post*, September 23, 2007. Retrieved August 2008 (http://www.washingtonpost.com/wp-dyn/content/article/2007/09/22/AR2007092201401.html).

Morse, Jane, "U.S. Foreign Aid Agency Joins with MTV to Fight Human Trafficking." U.S. Department of State, August 20, 2008. Retrieved August 28, 2008 (http://www.america.gov/st/hr-english/2008/August/20080820131755ajesrom0.6230585.html).

NBC News. "L.I. Woman Gets 11 Years in Domestic Slavery Case." WNBC News, June 26, 2008. Retrieved August 23,2008 (http://www.wnbc.com/news/16714910/detail.html).

Reckinger, Carole. "Burma's Forced Labour." *New Statesman*, June 9, 2008. Retrieved August 2008 (http://www.newstatesman.com/asia/2008/06/forced-labour-burma-work).

Reiss, Jana. "Abolitionist Teen Speaks Out Against Modern-Day Slavery." *Publishers Weekly*, February 21, 2002. Retrieved August 2008 (http://www.publishersweekly.com/article/CA6418085.html).

Rosenthal, Sharon. "Rockin' Against Slavery." *Jewish Journal*, April 30, 2003. Retrieved August 18, 2008 (http://www.jewishjournal.com/up_front/article/rockin_against_slavery_20030501).

"Slavery in the 21st Century." *New Internationalist*, August 2001. Retrieved August 16, 2008 (http://www.newint.org/issue337/facts.htm).

Sommer, Amy. "Modern-Day Slavery in America." University of Texas, 2004. Retrieved August 21, 2008 (http://www.utwatch.org/archives/issue/issue7_modernslavery.html).

Stickley, Paul. "Slavery in the Modern Era." World Socialist Web Site, 1999. Retrieved August 15, 2008 (http://www.wsws.org/articles/1999/sep1999/slav-s09.shtml).

Stowe, Harriet Beecher. *Uncle Tom's Cabin: or Life Among the Lowly*. Hartfordshire, England: Wordsworth Editions LTD, 1999.

Thomas, Pierre, Jack Date, and Theresa Cook. "Modern Day Slavery: Lucrative Trade Thriving." ABC News, May 22, 2007. Retrieved August 15, 2008 (http://abcnews.go.com/wn/story?id=3199772).

UN Office on Drugs and Crime. "United Nations General Assembly Urges Stronger Action Against Human Trafficking." June 4, 2008. Retrieved August 28, 2008 (http://www.unodc.org/unodc/en/frontpage/united-nations-general-assembly-urges-stronger-action-against-human-trafficking.html).

U.S. Agency for International Development. "Radiohead Joins USAID/MTV Campaign to Raise Awareness and Help Victims of Human Trafficking." April 30, 2008. Retrieved August 28, 2008 (http://www.usaid.gov/press/releases/2008/pr080430.html).

U.S. Department of Health and Human Services. "Fact Sheet: Trafficking Victims Protection Act of 2000." 2004. Retrieved August 17, 2008 (http://www.acf.hhs.gov/trafficking/about/TVPA_2000.html).

U.S. Department of Justice. "Department of Justice Issues T-Visa to Protect Women, Children, and All Victims of Human Trafficking." January 24, 2002. Retrieved August 23, 2008 (http://www.usdoj.gov/opa/pr/2002/January/02_crt_038.htm).

U.S. Department of State. "U.S. Government Efforts to Fight Demand Fueling Human Trafficking." Office to Monitor and Combat Trafficking in Persons, January 7, 2008. Retrieved August 23, 2008 (http://www.state.gov/g/tip/rls/fs/08/100208.htm).

U.S. Government Printing Office. "United States Code." 2008. Retrieved August 24, 2008 (http://www.gpoaccess.gov/USCODE/index.html).

Vickery, Martha. "Teens Take a Stand Against Human Trafficking." *Twin Cities Daily Planet*, July 17, 2008. Retrieved August 2008 (http://www.tcdailyplanet.net/article/2008/07/14/teens-take-stand-against-human-trafficking.html).

Index

About the Author

Linda Bickerstaff is a University of Missouri–trained general surgeon and a Mayo Clinic–trained peripheral vascular surgeon who has been writing magazine articles and books for teens since her retirement from surgical practice. She has written several books for Rosen Publishing and has learned a tremendous amount in researching each book.

Photo Credits

Designer: Tom Forget; Editor: Andrea Sclarow
Photo Researcher: Cindy Reiman